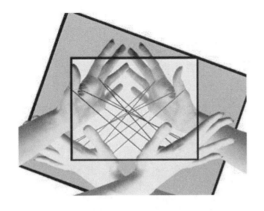

Bridge to the Classroom
ESL Cases for Teacher Exploration

TEACHER'S GUIDE

VOLUME 3. ADULT CONTEXTS

Joy Egbert and Gina Mikel Petrie

 T E S O L Teachers of English to Speakers of Other Languages, Inc.

Typeset in Sabon and Vag Rounded

by Capitol Communication Systems, Inc., Crofton, Maryland USA

and printed by United Graphics, Inc., Mattoon, Illinois USA

Teachers of English to Speakers of Other Languages, Inc.

700 South Washington Street, Suite 200

Alexandria, Virginia 22314 USA

Tel 703-836-0774 • Fax 703-836-6447 • E-mail publications@tesol.org • http://www.tesol.org/

Director of Publishing: Paul Gibbs

Managing Editor: Marilyn Kupetz

Copy Editor: Cheryl Duksta

Additional Reader: Sarah Duffy

Cover Design: Capitol Communication Systems, Inc.

ISBN 1931185239

For my favorite teachers ever—Gina Petrie,
Maura McCulloch, and Shayla Sivert.

— JE

For Mrs. Nettie Bellman, my second grade teacher,
for giving me my first glimpse of truly inspired
teaching. (And for believing that I really would
grow up to be Mayor someday.)

—GMP

Table of Contents

Acknowledgments

Thanks to the colleagues, friends, and teachers who supplied stories for this book. We especially thank Heidi Olson and Sheri Lattimore. We also extend our appreciation to the TESOL Publications Committee, especially Marilyn Kupetz, Julian Edge, and the fabulous copyeditors with whom they associate. The effort of Mila Trouteva made this book possible, as did the unwavering support of our families. In addition, Yu-Feng (Diana) Yang contributed greatly to two cases in this volume.

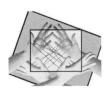

Concepts and Issues by Case

The adult cases cover some of the concepts and issues listed below. The cases may cover other concepts and issues that are not mentioned here.

Case	Title	Concepts	Issues
1	First Line of Defense	• language learning myths and misconceptions • interacting with colleagues • relationships between subject-area and ESL teachers • teacher perceptions and beliefs	• BICS/CALP • critical period • role of mainstream teachers • language in context • cultural stereotypes • family involvement • length of time to learn a second language • code-switching • expectations and achievement
2	Listen to Me	• oral skills • teaching techniques • working within boundaries	• total physical response • teacher review • newcomers • games for language learning • authentic activities • learning motivation
3	Exchanges	• cultural and background differences • teaching integrated skills • scaffolding	• using native language in the classroom • how skills relate to each other • factors that influence a student's language abilities • locating information on student's background • designing interactions in the classroom • scaffolding a student's weaker skills with stronger ones • managing different language levels in the classroom • gender differences

(continued on page x)

Case	Title	Concepts	Issues
4	Culture Clash	• cultural and background differences • classroom management	• teacher expectations • teacher attitude • legal responsibilities • discipline
5	Who Am I?	• culture shock	• learner perceptions • information sources • learners as representatives of their culture • culturally responsive teaching, stereotyping
6	Voicing an Opinion	• classroom management • teaching in special contexts	• designing interaction • using realia in the classroom • appropriate assessment • using native language in the classroom • grammar learning
7	Restructuring Ideas	• grammar teaching and learning	• adapting materials • integrating skills • teaching-assessment relationship • using technology to support language learning • building curriculum • noticing • communicative language teaching • inductive vs. deductive learning
8	Standards of English	• standard English • oral language teaching and learning	• authentic activities • BICS/CALP • working with migrant populations • order of skills taught • learning centers

(continued on page xi)

Case	Title	Concepts	Issues
9	Reading Between the Lines	• reading • language and content • learning strategies	• reflective teaching practices • time management • skills integration • changing non-ESL teachers' practices • strategic (and communicative) competence • BICS/CALP • language of academic texts
10	The Subject of Language	• English language learners' writing • 6+1 traits • genres	• writing goals • students as models • using technology to support language learning
11	Solving a Mystery	• technology in language learning • adult learners	• interaction between nonnative speakers of English • critical thinking • metacognition • student perceptions
12	A Process of Evaluation	• English for specific purposes • standardized assessment • mandated assessment • assessment goals • types of assessment • impact of assessment	• matching teaching with testing • authenticity of assessment • funding for assessment • characteristics of good assessments • decision-making • test bias
13	Homework	• classroom inquiry • culture	• professional networking • community, family, and teacher relationships
14	So-Called Expert	• demographics • ESL programs	• data gathering • program choices • skills vs. themes
15	Create Your Own Case		

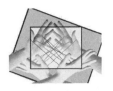

Introduction

Teachers who can analyze and handle the variety of contexts and problems that arise in their English as a second language (ESL) classrooms will be more effective in reducing conflict and helping their students learn than those without such preparation. To prepare teachers to face authentic classroom situations, teacher education programs need to use methods that promote creativity, the ability to think critically, resourcefulness, and independence, while encouraging teacher education students to make links between theories of learning and actual classroom practice. Lecture and other noninteractive teaching methods have typically not been very successful in facilitating these goals. In the case method, the teacher asks students to research, analyze, and solve classroom dilemmas.

BENEFITS OF THE CASE METHOD

Reality-based cases that are open ended, such as the ones in this volume, stimulate discussion and help teacher education students examine their knowledge, experiences, attitudes, and skills.

In addition, cases can help teachers to

- sharpen their overall communication skills, including their overall ability to listen critically and with empathy, to read with a purpose, to synthesize information, to make inferences, to discuss serious issues with colleagues, and to speak more clearly and persuasively
- refine their interpersonal and cooperative learning skills
- learn how to handle their emotions and conflict more easily and build positively on the ideas of others
- understand and accept ideas different from their own
- understand some of the challenges of working with students, parents, and colleagues from diverse cultures in demanding and confusing situations
- narrow the gap between theory and practice
- expose students to a wide variety of teaching situations
- begin to think like language teachers. (Jackson, 1999, pp. 59–60)

Another benefit of the case method is that it requires teacher educators to familiarize themselves with recent literature in the field and with principles and practices of ESL classroom teaching events (which they may not have experienced for some time).

DISADVANTAGES OF THE CASE METHOD

A disadvantage of the case method is that it takes time and effort to become familiar with recent literature and practice. Teaching effectively with cases also requires instructors to study and practice. However, many books and articles exist to help. In addition, reality-based cases for specific ESL teacher audiences are difficult to find. The volumes that do exist contain cases that are either too brief and written for too diverse an audience or have the solutions provided, thereby removing many of the opportunities that the case method offers. Cases written for other fields or for general teacher education may be useful in ESL teacher education, but language teacher educators must revise and adapt these to fit specific teaching situations and problems from authentic language teaching contexts.

Despite these disadvantages, the benefits of using the case method in ESL teacher education are definitely worth the time and effort that teacher educators must expend to use it well.

THE CASES

Teacher education students who do not have experience with ESL students usually struggle with how to teach because they do not have knowledge of authentic ESL classroom situations. Because language learning classroom situations are very different at the elementary, secondary, and adult levels, the same basic issues, and the contextual differences among the three levels of education, are addressed in three different volumes. Adapting classroom situations from one level to another is a very difficult task for teacher education students; breaking the content into the three volumes allows situations to be accurately addressed.

Because the parallel case studies in the three volumes address the same issues of second language learning and teaching at different levels, classroom discussion is not only possible but is enriched in classrooms where teacher education students are certifying at different levels and using the different volumes. In fact, teacher education students will have the opportunity to learn about ESL students in other levels and will be able to discuss teaching objectives and goals from a wide range of teaching situations.

The cases in all of the volumes are based on situations that we have personally experienced or that were related to us by colleagues. They can be used in any order, and each lends itself to a variety of issues, activities, and products. Guidelines, readings, and possible outcomes are suggested in the teacher's guide rather than in the texts because we firmly believe that it is important not only to give the instructor options of how and what to present but also that an important aspect of the case method is that students be allowed to reflect without influences, at least at first. This leads to independence and opportunities for critical thinking and development of students' questions and strategies.

USING THIS GUIDE

This teacher's guide provides suggestions and examples for using the adult-level text of the *Bridge to the Classroom* series. It starts by presenting the case process, including a general outline of steps for teachers and students to follow in working with cases. It then addresses each case separately, presenting possible solutions, several resources, activities, and ideas for each step in the process.

For each case the guidelines, readings, and sample responses are offered as general suggestions; not nearly all of the possibilities are (or could be) presented here. For this reason, we have included space for teacher notes at the end of each case description. Questions and issues overlap between some of the cases to show how the issues can present in different ways and also to provide additional practice working with these issues. In addition, new vocabulary terms are not always explained in the text; ideally, students will be seekers of information rather than passive receivers.

THE CASE PROCESS

There are many approaches to using cases in education. The most successful case teachers use some variation of the steps below. Although following this process exactly is not required, we recommend that teachers new to the case method follow these steps as closely as possible until they understand the method. Space has been provided in the student books for students to make notes next to the case text and for them to answer the case analysis questions. For the first iteration, the instructor should monitor the students as they proceed through each of the case method steps, answering questions, suggesting directions for students to follow, and modeling how answers will be weighed.

Each case is followed by a set of similar questions that encourage students to reflect on the steps.

STEP 1. IDENTIFY THE ISSUES

The students should brainstorm the issues in groups, deciding which facts of the case are relevant, which are urgent, and which are neither. Rather than taking the case at face value, students should think critically about the possible reasons for the concerns expressed by the people in the case and also about factors that may play a role in finding a solution. This is the most important, yet also the most difficult, step in problem solving. Students should be given sufficient time and provided with enough interaction to clarify the issues to the extent possible.

In the cases, the following questions address this step:

1. What problems or questions are the stakeholders facing?
2. What seem to be the obvious causes?
3. What might be some underlying or less obvious causes?
4. What other issues seem to be relevant?
5. How are these issues relevant to language teaching?

STEP 2. CONSIDER ALL PERSPECTIVES

Students should list any stakeholders, both obvious and less explicit. They can mention time frames, circumstances, and causes that apply to each stakeholder. In the cases, the following questions address this step:

1. Who is directly affected by the issues? How are they affected?
2. Who directly affects the issues? How?
3. What might be some of the stakeholders' thoughts and assumptions about the issues?
4. Who else might be affected by the issues? Who else might affect the issues? How?

STEP 3. IDENTIFY RELEVANT PROFESSIONAL KNOWLEDGE

Students should review the relevant literature. The instructor can point out appropriate readings in the student books and other resources for each case or ask students to discover and share their own resources. The questions for this step vary because they directly address the professional knowledge needed to resolve each case's specific issues.

STEP 4. CONSIDER POSSIBLE ACTIONS AND CONSEQUENCES

Students should note likely and unlikely actions, and they should articulate the reasons behind each action that they project. They should examine the consequences of each action and how they might affect the stakeholders in the long and short terms. An extensive discussion, in large or small groups, is essential to this step. Although they may vary in each case, the following questions can help:

1. What action is most likely to help each of the stakeholders in this situation?
2. What other actions would you recommend?
3. What decision should the stakeholders make? Why?
4. What other actions should the stakeholders take immediately and during the next school year? Why?

STEP 5. QUESTIONS FOR REFLECTION

The instructor should assist the students in bringing the case to closure. This can include, for example, summarizing the students' findings, having students reflect on the process, voting on better solutions, debriefing on specific criteria, or inviting guests (e.g., school administrators, in-service teachers) to adjudicate. Each case includes reflection questions the teacher can use to link the case issues to students' backgrounds and experiences or to extend the discussion. Final products can range from a written case analysis to a role-play or a video production. Suggestions for products are presented in this guide for each case.

Case 1. First Line of Defense

IDENTIFY THE ISSUES

MAJOR ISSUES

Language learning myths and misconceptions, interactions with colleagues, relationships between subject-area and ESL teachers, teacher perceptions and beliefs

OTHER ISSUES

Basic interpersonal communicative skills and cognitive academic language proficiency (BICS/ CALP), critical period, role of mainstream teachers, language in context, cultural stereotypes, family involvement, length of time to learn a second language, code-switching, expectations, achievement

READINGS

The following readings, also listed in each volume's Case Resources section, can help students understand the case issues. The Case Resources section contains many other texts that can also inform students.

Cary, S. (2000). *Working with second language learners: Answers to teachers' top ten questions.* Portsmouth, NH: Heinemann.

Cummins, J. (2003). *Basic interpersonal communicative skills and cognitive academic language proficiency: BICS and CALP* [Web site]. Belmont, MA: i teach i learn.com. Retrieved February 5, 2005, from http://www.iteachilearn.com/cummins/bicscalp.html

McLaughlin, B. (1992). *Myths and misconceptions about second language learning: What every teacher needs to unlearn* (Educational Practice Report No. 5). Santa Cruz, CA: University of California, National Center for Research on Cultural Diversity and Second Language Learning. Retrieved February 5, 2005, from http://www.ncela.gwu.edu/pubs/ncrcdsll/epr5.htm

Samway, K., & McKeon, D. (1999). *Myths and realities: Best practices for language minority students.* Portsmouth, NH: Heinemann.

DISCUSS THE ISSUES

Positive Aspects
- The teacher is thinking and talking about the issues and is open to discussion.
- The teacher is well informed.
- The students are aware and concerned.
- The prior teacher used context-based language techniques, so the students are used to these techniques.

Negative Aspects
- Because the teacher is new to the school, she does not have a history in the position and has limited political and personal knowledge of colleagues.

- Some subject-area teachers already feel some resentment because they expect the new teacher to be different and better than the last teacher.
- Colleagues hold opinions that are personally important to them and that they will not relinquish easily.

Questions to Consider
- Why are the teachers gossiping? Is this their way of showing concern?
- How do the teachers feel about ESL education? How do they feel about ESL students?
- Who is ultimately responsible for educating ESL students?
- Why is communication so poor about these students?

CONSIDER ALL PERSPECTIVES

Students might mention the perspectives of the teacher, the teacher's colleagues, and the ESL students. Indirect stakeholders include the state, the school, and possibly the families of the English language learners.

IDENTIFY RELEVANT PROFESSIONAL KNOWLEDGE

Students can refer to the readings mentioned previously, ESL methods texts, articles and books on myths and misconceptions about ESL education, and second language acquisition (SLA) texts and articles.

CONSIDER POSSIBLE ACTIONS AND CONSEQUENCES

The teacher in this case could take some or none of the following actions and suffer some or none of the following consequences:

Action	Consequences
Agree with colleagues just to fit in.	Nothing changes.
Bow out of the discussion politely.	The teacher is allowed time to think and can act later.
Postpone the discussion until after the teacher has had time to think about it.	The teacher is allowed time to think and can act later.
Launch into an explanation of misconceptions about second language learning (tactfully or defensively), thus acting as an educating agent.	The teacher educates colleagues.
	The teacher polarizes colleagues.
	The discussion alienates the teacher.
Ask for a transfer from the school.	The teacher postpones the confrontation.
	The teacher does not help her students.
	The teacher's colleagues do not get educated.

The teacher goes about her business and slowly educates colleagues.	Students and colleagues benefit.
	Colleagues become resentful.
	Subject-area teachers become resentful and take out their resentment on ESL students.
Ask the principal for permission to present a workshop for subject-area teachers.	Teachers do not attend and nothing changes.
	Teachers get educated.
	The discussion polarizes faculty.

The teacher also might tell colleagues that she would like to share information with anyone who wants to stop by her classroom, she might invite teachers to conference about the students they have in common, and she might get ESL students' families more involved in the school and program.

CLOSURE: QUESTIONS FOR REFLECTION
- Summarize the class's analysis of the case.
- Present questions for current or future reflection. (See the case book for Reflection Questions.)

SUGGESTED ACTIVITIES
These activities can be used individually or together.

WRITE A CASE ANALYSIS
Following the questions at the end of the case, students analyze the case and prepare a written analysis prior to discussion in class. Students can work in teams or individually.

ROLE-PLAY
Videotape a role-play and have students analyze it later in the semester. Students may role-play the case as it is written in the text, choosing a variety of extensions or endings, or they may choose to carry out the themes of the case by role-playing a discussion between an ESL teacher and one of the following people:

- a colleague who does not understand why the ESL teacher isn't teaching using audiolingualism and grammar translation (the way the colleague learned a foreign language)
- a native-English-speaking student who wants to know why ESL students get credit for playing games and having fun when he must do serious work
- the ESL teacher's aunt, who tells the teacher that she thinks immigrant adults are slow learners
- a program director who is worried about raising the school's TOEFL test scores and is concerned about English language learners' progress

COLLABORATE WITH IN-SERVICE TEACHERS

Ask each student to confer about the case individually with a teacher in a local community college. If the local college cannot accommodate this request, students may confer with instructors in another adult ESL program or through e-mail with teachers at a distance. Have half of the students confer with subject-area instructors in the partner institution, discussing the teachers' concerns about having ESL students in their classrooms. Discuss what teachers do to help their ESL students and how they cooperate with other instructors to help their ESL students achieve. Have the other half of the students confer with ESL instructors in the partner institution and discuss the case with them. They should discuss whether and how they cooperate with the subject-area instructors to help their ESL students. Have students discuss what they learned with the whole class and apply it to the case issues.

COMPLETE A SUPPLEMENTAL WORKSHEET

Have students complete the supplemental activity worksheet on the next page. This can happen either before they have analyzed the case or after the case analysis is complete. Students then introduce themselves as language learners to each other and reflect on what they have learned from this brief activity.

SUPPLEMENTAL ACTIVITY WORKSHEET, CASE 1

INSTRUCTIONS

Complete the following survey. Then, answer the reflection question.

Survey

My native language is _____ .

In this language I can (check all that apply)

_____Listen to and understand a lecture about forestry.

_____Ask someone what time it is.

_____Read and understand a newspaper economics article.

_____Write a grocery list.

_____Listen to and understand a story about a trip.

_____Give a presentation on my views of education so far.

_____Read and understand signs in a bus station.

_____Write a cause/effect paper using resources.

My second language is _____ .

In this language I can (check all that apply)

_____Read and understand a menu.

_____Write a summary of a journal article.

_____Take part in a formal debate on politics in education.

_____Listen to and understand a clerk in a store.

_____Write a very short note to a friend.

_____Read and understand a history textbook.

_____Give someone directions to the grocery store.

_____Listen to and understand a lecture about physics.

My third language is _____ .

In this language I can (check all that apply)

_____Listen to and understand a discussion about the media.

_____Ask someone for help in a store.

_____Read and understand a train schedule.

_____Write a persuasive paper about affirmative action.

_____Listen to and understand a description of a menu.

_____Speak in front of an audience about educational equality.

_____Read and understand a journal article on sociology.

_____Write a note requesting a hotel room reservation.

Reflection Question

As I look at my abilities in these languages, what I notice is

NOTES ON CASE 1

Case 2. Listen to Me

IDENTIFY THE ISSUES

MAJOR ISSUES
Teaching oral skills, teaching techniques, working within boundaries

OTHER ISSUES
Total physical response (TPR), teacher review, newcomers, games for language learning, authentic activities, learning motivation

READINGS
The following readings, also listed in each volume's Case Resources section, can help students understand the case issues. The Case Resources section contains many other texts that can also inform students.

Bailey, K., & Savage, L. (Ed.). (1994). *New ways in teaching speaking.* Alexandria, VA: TESOL.

Larsen-Freeman, D. (2000). *Techniques and principles in language teaching* (3rd ed.). Oxford, England: Oxford University Press.

Ray, B., & Seely, C. (1998). *Fluency through TPR storytelling* (2nd ed.). Berkeley, CA: Command Performance Institute.

Romijn, E., & Seely, C. (1997). *Live action English: A total physical response student/teacher text* (Millennium ed.). Berkeley, CA: Command Performance Institute.

DISCUSS THE ISSUES

Positive Aspects
- The assistant director is willing to listen to the teacher.
- The teacher has a chance to reflect on his teaching techniques.
- Students seem motivated, and the content is authentic for them.

Negative Aspects
- The assistant director is questioning the teacher's classroom authority.
- The teacher has to take time to prepare an explanation of his method.
- Not everyone believes that TPR is a useful technique (or can use it well).

CONSIDER ALL PERSPECTIVES
Students might mention the perspectives of ESL students, the teacher, the administrator, and possibly the program.

IDENTIFY RELEVANT PROFESSIONAL KNOWLEDGE
Students can refer to the readings mentioned previously, ESL methods texts, articles and books on listening and speaking skills and teaching beginners, and adult program policies for teacher review.

CONSIDER POSSIBLE ACTIONS AND CONSEQUENCES

The teacher could take some or none of the following actions and suffer some or none of the following consequences.

Action	Consequences
Tell Mr. Kantor that the teacher will change his technique to a more traditional listening and speaking one.	Students lose interest. The teacher loses interest. Mr. Kantor is satisfied that standards are being met.
Carefully explain the rationale behind TPR to Mr. Kantor.	Mr. Kantor agrees to this technique because it meets the standards. Mr. Kantor does not agree and asks the teacher to change his technique.
Ask Mr. Kantor to observe another part of the TPR process.	Mr. Kantor gets a better overall idea of the process. The teacher has another chance to show what he is doing to meet goals.
The teacher tells Mr. Kantor that he needs to do as he sees fit in his classroom.	Mr. Kantor warns or fires him. The students lose their teacher. The teacher loses his job or the goodwill of the administration.

CLOSURE: QUESTIONS FOR REFLECTION
- Summarize the class's analysis of the case.
- Present questions for current or future reflection. (See the case book for Reflection Questions.)

SUGGESTED ACTIVITIES

These activities can be used individually or together.

CREATE A TPR LESSON OR VIDEO

Students find or create a TPR lesson and teach other students in the class, or they watch a TPR video and analyze the lesson.

CREATE LISTENING MINILESSONS

Students present listening minilessons to peers.

ROLE-PLAY

Students role-play the meeting between Mr. Kantor and the teacher.

Case 3. Exchanges

IDENTIFY THE ISSUES

MAJOR ISSUES
Cultural and other background differences, teaching integrated skills, scaffolding

OTHER ISSUES
Allowing or prohibiting native language in the classroom, relating skills to each other, identifying factors that influence a student's language abilities, locating information on students' backgrounds, designing interactions in the classroom, scaffolding a student's weaker skills with stronger ones, managing different language levels within the classroom, addressing gender differences

READINGS
The following readings, also listed in each volume's Case Resources section, can help students understand the case issues. The Case Resources section contains many other texts that can also inform students.

Brown, H. D. (2001). *Teaching by principles: An interactive approach to language pedagogy.* White Plains, NY: Longman.

Garcia, E. (2002). *Student cultural diversity: Understanding and meeting the challenge* (3rd ed.). Boston: Houghton Mifflin.

Gersten, R., & Jimenez, R. (1998). *Promoting learning for culturally and linguistically diverse students.* Belmont, CA: Wadsworth.

DISCUSS THE ISSUES

Positive Aspects
- Intercultural interaction helps learners interact in the target language.
- Peers can be resources for each other.
- Practice helps learners and teachers.
- First-day activities can be crucial in establishing the classroom's learning climate.

Negative Aspects
- Students may need time to understand each other.
- Assigning groups without knowing the students can create problems.
- Teachers can begin to feel too comfortable and forget that situations change.
- Students need to understand the teacher's and the course's goals and how each activity relates to those goals.
- Learners study for different reasons that the teacher must recognize and perhaps address.

CONSIDER ALL PERSPECTIVES
Students might mention the perspectives of ESL students, the teacher, and the program.

IDENTIFY RELEVANT PROFESSIONAL KNOWLEDGE

Students can refer to the readings mentioned previously, ESL methods texts, articles and books on culture and cultural perspectives on education, and warm-up activities and lessons.

CONSIDER POSSIBLE ACTIONS AND CONSEQUENCES

The teacher could take some or none of the following actions and suffer some or none of the following consequences.

Action	Consequences
Allow students to work within their culture groups only.	Learners miss opportunities to learn from students different from themselves.
	Learners can speak their native language more often (both an advantage and a disadvantage).
	Stereotypes and other misunderstandings result.
	Students do not have as much help with their weaknesses.
	Learners are happier in class.
Prepare different lessons for different abilities.	The teacher meets the different needs of the students (though she needs more time and effort to do so).
	Learners cannot work together as well.
	Learners interpret different lessons as bias in some way.
Take more time to help the students get to know each other.	The teacher takes time away from mandated curriculum and test preparation.
	Standards are not directly addressed.
	Students are more willing to work together.
	Students are more prepared for authentic situations outside of class.
Do some research before making a decision. For example, find out more about students' backgrounds and cultures.	The teacher makes more informed decisions.
	The research takes time but does not solve the immediate problem.

CLOSURE: QUESTIONS FOR REFLECTION

- Summarize the class's analysis of the case.
- Present questions for current or future reflection. (See the case book for Reflection Questions.)

SUGGESTED ACTIVITIES

These activities can be used individually or together.

EVALUATE PEER RESPONSES

Students evaluate their peers' responses to the case.

ROLE-PLAY

Two student groups research the culture of one of the groups from the case and then dialogue from the perspective of the culture they have studied.

INVITE GUEST SPEAKERS

Invite guest speakers from each of the culture groups represented in the case. Have these guests present their perspectives on the case.

TEACH ICEBREAKERS AND WARM-UPS

Students find and teach icebreakers and warm-up activities to their peers.

Case 4. Culture Clash

IDENTIFY THE ISSUES

MAJOR ISSUES
Cultural and other background differences, classroom management

OTHER ISSUES
Teacher expectations, teacher attitude, legal responsibilities, discipline

READINGS
The following readings, also listed in each volume's Case Resources section, can help students understand the case issues. The Case Resources section contains many other texts that can also inform students.

Barbieri, M. (2002). *"Change my life forever": Giving voice to English language learners.* Portsmouth, NH: Heinemann.

Díaz-Rico, L. (2004). *Teaching English learners: Strategies and methods.* Boston: Allyn & Bacon.

Peitzman, F., & Gadda, G. (1994). *With different eyes: Insights into teaching language minority students across the disciplines.* New York: Longman.

DISCUSS THE ISSUES

Positive Aspects
- The students' respect for the teacher made the students easier for her to deal with.
- The teacher made it clear that she expected them to behave differently.
- The incident seemed to be over after the men went back inside the classroom.

Negative Aspects
- The other students are waiting to see what the teacher will do about this serious situation.
- The Israeli and Palestinian students seem to be exposed to politics outside of school that affect their school behavior.
- The teacher may be obligated to report the situation to the administration.

CONSIDER ALL PERSPECTIVES
Students might mention the perspectives of the two ESL students, the teacher, and the class. Other stakeholders include the administration, which has a vested interest in classroom discipline.

IDENTIFY RELEVANT PROFESSIONAL KNOWLEDGE
Students can refer to the readings mentioned previously, classroom management texts, and articles and books on culture and cultural perspectives on education, legal responsibilities of teachers, and teacher expectations.

CONSIDER POSSIBLE ACTIONS AND CONSEQUENCES

The teacher could take some or none of the following actions and suffer some or none of the following consequences.

Action	Consequences
Take the young men to the program office immediately after class.	The teacher can discipline the students but runs the risk of not understanding the problem.
	She can document the process in case another problem occurs.
	The young men are suspended and miss more class.
Discuss the incident with the class.	The teacher embarrasses the young men.
	The students in the class take sides and exacerbate the problem.
	The teacher conducts a just-in-time lesson.
Talk to an administrator before making a decision.	Although getting an appointment takes time, the teacher is following protocol and would protect herself from liability.
	The administrator is likely to suspend the students without question.
Talk to the young men individually after class.	The teacher finds out the real reason for their argument.
	The teacher makes the problem worse.
	The young men release some pressure they feel and are truly sorry.

CLOSURE: QUESTIONS FOR REFLECTION
- Summarize the class's analysis of the case.
- Present questions for current or future reflection. (See the case book for Reflection Questions.)

SUGGESTED ACTIVITIES

These activities can be used individually or together.

ROLE-PLAY

Role-play the teacher talking to the administrator or the teacher talking to the young men individually.

READ ENGLISH-LANGUAGE NEWSPAPERS

Read some of the English-language newspapers from other cultures and reflect on the views that they support.

INTERVIEW TEACHERS AND STUDENTS

Interview a teacher to find out how he or she gains the respect of adult students. Students might also interview adult students to see what makes them respect their teachers.

Case 5. Who Am I?

IDENTIFY THE ISSUES

MAJOR ISSUE
Culture shock

OTHER ISSUES
Learner perceptions, information sources, culturally responsive teaching

READINGS
The following readings, also listed in each volume's Case Resources section, can help students understand the case issues. The Case Resources section contains many other texts that can also inform students.

Auerbach, E. (1997). *Making meaning, making change.* McHenry, IL: Delta Systems.

Brown, H. D. (2001). *Teaching by principles: An interactive approach to language pedagogy.* White Plains, NY: Longman.

Burnette, J. (1999). *Critical behaviors and strategies for teaching culturally diverse students.* Arlington, VA: ERIC Clearinghouse on Disabilities and Gifted Education. (EC Digest No. E584). Retrieved February 5, 2005, from http://ericec.org/digests/e584.html

DISCUSS THE ISSUES

Positive Aspects
- The student trusts the teacher enough to confide in her.
- The student understands some of the sources, if not the effects, of his problem.
- The student wants to fit in despite his difficulties.
- The teacher realizes many of the underlying causes of the problems.

Negative Aspects
- The student needs help and answers immediately, but the teacher needs to think more about her actions.
- The student does not mention whether his family is aware of his problems.
- The teacher does not know which of her perceptions of the student are accurate.

CONSIDER ALL PERSPECTIVES
Students might mention the perspectives of the student, the teacher, and the family. Petya might be indirectly involved.

IDENTIFY RELEVANT PROFESSIONAL KNOWLEDGE
Students can refer to the readings mentioned previously, ESL methods texts, and articles and books on culture shock, culturally responsive teaching, and the needs of adult students and how to meet them.

CONSIDER POSSIBLE ACTIONS AND CONSEQUENCES

The teacher could take some or none of the following actions and suffer some or none of the following consequences.

Action	Consequences
Tell the student to talk to his family.	The family members are in the same position and do not know what to do.
	They may be able to help if they understand the problems.
	They are not able to help solve the issues with the ESL class.
Work with the whole class on culture issues.	The student's specific problems are not addressed.
	All the students understand the process of living in a new culture.
Find a buddy to help the student with questions about culture.	The student is given someone to count on and turn to for help.
	The student feels that the teacher is abdicating responsibility.
	If the buddy is another student, the information might not be reliable.
Tell the student it is normal to feel culture shock and that he will get over it as he adjusts.	This concept might not be true.
	The teacher avoids considering the real, immediate needs of the student.
	The student realizes he is not alone in his feelings.

CLOSURE: QUESTIONS FOR REFLECTION
- Summarize the class's analysis of the case.
- Present questions for current or future reflection. (See the case book for Reflection Questions.)

SUGGESTED ACTIVITIES
These activities can be used individually or together.

WORK THROUGH CULTURE SHOCK
Students list ways to work with students through different stages of culture shock.

DEVELOP CULTURALLY SENSITIVE LESSON PLANS

Students review lesson plans and reflect on how they could be more culturally responsive.

RESEARCH LOCAL SERVICES

Students describe types of local services available to help adult nonresident students. To whom would you refer Abekeh? Why?

Case 6. Voicing an Opinion

IDENTIFY THE ISSUES

MAJOR ISSUES

Classroom management, teaching in special contexts

OTHER ISSUES

Designing interaction, using realia, learning grammar, assessing appropriately, using native language

READINGS

The following readings, also listed in each volume's Case Resources section, can help students understand the case issues. The Case Resources section contains many other texts that can also inform students.

Andrews, L. (2001). English and usage. In *Linguistics for L2 teachers* (pp. 37–56). Mahwah, NJ: Lawrence Erlbaum.

Larsen-Freeman, D. (2000). *Techniques and principles in language teaching* (3rd ed.). Oxford, England: Oxford University Press.

Lewis, M. (1996). *Using student-centered methods with teacher-centered ESL students*. Toronto, Ontario, Canada: Pippin.

DISCUSS THE ISSUES

Positive Aspects
- The teacher has some ideas about principles of second language acquisition that she uses to guide her activities.
- She tries to involve all of the students.
- She understands that she needs to create opportunities for interaction.

Negative Aspects
- There are huge barriers to interaction.
- Designing interactions that overcome these barriers might take more time and effort than it is worth.

CONSIDER ALL PERSPECTIVES

Students might mention the perspectives of the ESL students and the teacher. The other teachers and the prison administration also have a vested interest.

IDENTIFY RELEVANT PROFESSIONAL KNOWLEDGE

Students can refer to the readings mentioned previously, ESL methods texts, articles and books on teaching ESL in prison, and texts and articles that focus on interaction.

CONSIDER POSSIBLE ACTIONS AND CONSEQUENCES

The teacher could take some or none of the following actions and suffer some or none of the following consequences.

Action	Consequences
Find out more about creating effective opportunities for interaction in language classrooms.	The teacher makes more informed decisions. This requires the teacher's time and effort. Students must wait.
Investigate other ways for teaching grammar and writing.	The teacher makes more informed decisions. There may be effective ways to teach that do not require one-on-one interaction. This takes the teacher's time and effort.
Research the backgrounds of the students to find out more about how they might be grouped.	The teacher has the opportunity to speak with students. Not all information is available for the students. The teacher discovers that there is no way to group the students, wasting time and effort.
Keep doing things the way they are done currently.	Students do not have opportunities for optimal language learning. The administrator prefers this option. The teacher's job is easier.

CLOSURE: QUESTIONS FOR REFLECTION
- Summarize the class's analysis of the case.
- Present questions for current or future reflection. (See the case book for Reflection Questions.)

SUGGESTED ACTIVITIES

These activities can be used individually or together.

TEACH A LESSON TWO WAYS

Students design and teach a lesson. They teach it once without any student interaction and once with interaction, reflecting on the differences.

ROLE-PLAY

Students role-play students with characteristics that the instructor provides. Among themselves, students devise a seating chart for the simulated class that would lead to the least problems and the best chance for effective interaction.

REVISE A LESSON

Students revise a lesson—making as few changes as possible—that they believe would result in the largest student gains. Students justify their changes.

NOTES ON CASE 6

Case 7. Restructuring Ideas

IDENTIFY THE ISSUE

MAJOR ISSUES

Grammar teaching and learning

OTHER ISSUES

Material adaptation, skill integration, teaching-assessment relationship, role of technology, curriculum building, noticing, communicative language teaching, inductive versus deductive learning

READINGS

The following readings, also listed in each volume's Case Resources section, can help students understand the case issues. The Case Resources section contains many other texts that can also inform students.

Dubin, F., & Olshtain, E. (1987). *Course design: Developing programs and materials for language learning.* London: Cambridge University Press.

Egbert, J., & Hanson-Smith, E. (Eds.). (1999). *CALL environments: Research, practice, and critical issues.* Alexandria, VA: TESOL.

Pennington, M. (Ed.). (1995). *New ways in teaching grammar.* Alexandria, VA: TESOL.

DISCUSS THE ISSUES

Positive Aspects
- The teacher has resources to fall back on and materials are available.
- The administration seems supportive.
- Technology is available and will be useful.
- The teacher has leeway in what can be done.

Negative Aspects
- Creating something new will cost the teacher much time and effort.
- The books do not seem to consider individual students' needs.
- The teacher seems to be expected to teach to the TOEFL.

CONSIDER ALL PERSPECTIVES

Students might mention the perspectives of the ESL students and the teacher. The administrator is also affected and affects the issues.

IDENTIFY RELEVANT PROFESSIONAL KNOWLEDGE

Students can refer to the readings mentioned previously, ESL methods texts, articles and books on grammar teaching, and research on the acquisition of grammar.

CONSIDER POSSIBLE ACTIONS AND CONSEQUENCES

The teacher could take some or none of the following actions and suffer some or none of the following consequences.

Action	Consequences
Refuse to use the books.	The teacher is fired, reprimanded, or taken out of the class.
	The students benefit.
Focus on drill and practice.	The teacher does not meet individual students' needs.
	The teacher does not help students learn to communicate.
	The teacher helps students memorize the structures.
Work on adapting the lessons in the text.	The teacher may have difficulty finishing the prescribed curriculum.
	The teacher helps meet students' needs and styles.
Work with colleagues who have taught the class.	The teacher understands the goals and outcomes.
	The teacher gets ideas for activities.
	The teachers' colleagues expend time and effort.

CLOSURE: QUESTIONS FOR REFLECTION
- Summarize the class's analysis of the case.
- Present questions for current or future reflection. (See the case book for Reflection Questions.)

SUGGESTED ACTIVITIES

These activities can be used individually or together.

ADAPT MATERIALS TO MULTIPLE LEARNING STYLES

Students take a lesson, unit, or exercise from a grammar text and adapt it so that it is communicative and addresses multiple learning styles.

REVIEW GRAMMAR TEXTS AND SOFTWARE

Students develop a rubric and then review grammar texts or software, describing the advantages and disadvantages of each.

DEVELOP OR TAKE GRAMMAR TESTS

Students develop a communicative grammar test, or they take an online grammar test at an ESL Web site and reflect on their performance.

Case 8. Standards of English

IDENTIFY THE ISSUES

MAJOR ISSUES
Standard English, oral language teaching and learning

OTHER ISSUES
Authentic activities, BICS and CALP, migrant populations, order of skills instruction, resource search, learning center use

READINGS
The following readings, also listed in each volume's Case Resources section, can help students understand the case issues. The Case Resources section contains many other texts that can also inform students.

Andrews, L. (1998). *Language exploration and awareness: A resource book for teachers* (2nd ed.). Mahwah, NJ: Lawrence Erlbaum.

Cummins, J. (2003). *Basic interpersonal communicative skills and cognitive academic language proficiency: BICS and CALP* [Web site]. Belmont, MA: i teach i learn.com. Retrieved February 5, 2005, from http://www.iteachilearn.com/cummins/bicscalp.html

Ernst, G. (1994). "Talking Circle": Conversation and negotiation in the ESL classroom. *TESOL Quarterly, 28,* 293–322.

Narrish, J. (1997). english or English? Attitudes, local varieties and English language training. *TESL-EJ, 3*(1). Retrieved February 5, 2005, from http://www-writing.berkeley.edu/TESL-EJ /ej09/a2.html

DISCUSS THE ISSUES

Positive Aspects
- The teacher is trying to meet students' needs inside and outside of class.
- The teacher is using authentic tasks.
- The variety of activities helps address students' varying learning styles.

Negative Aspects
- The teacher seems to believe that standard English exists.
- Changing demographics make it difficult to design a set curriculum.
- The teacher is avoiding idioms and slang, which are important parts of the language.

CONSIDER ALL PERSPECTIVES

Students might mention the perspectives of the ESL students and the teacher. The organization, employers, and migrant communities might also be affected.

IDENTIFY RELEVANT PROFESSIONAL KNOWLEDGE

Students can refer to the readings mentioned previously, ESL methods texts, articles and books on oral language and standard English, and texts on the lives of immigrant and migrant children.

CONSIDER POSSIBLE ACTIONS AND CONSEQUENCES

The teacher could take some or none of the following actions and suffer some or none of the following consequences.

Action	Consequences
Stop the centers and use teacher-fronted drills.	The teacher does not address different learning styles.
	The drills require more of the teacher's time, with less individual interaction.
	The class is easier to manage.
	The teacher gives learners the impression that there is one correct way to speak.
	Some students learn better this way.
Learn more about the issues.	Nothing changes in the meantime.
	Better decisions are made.
Change goals and stop looking for a perfect standard language.	Learners understand that their interlanguage is acceptable.
	A variety of models and more authentic language are used in class.
	Standards are lowered for students.

QUESTIONS FOR REFLECTION
- Summarize the class's analysis of the case.
- Present questions for current or future reflection. (See the case book for Reflection Questions.)

SUGGESTED ACTIVITIES

These activities can be used individually or together.

CREATE ORAL DIALOGUE JOURNALS

Students learn and practice using oral dialogue journals. They can pair with another student in their class or with a language student from another class. They should review their tapes to reflect on how they model, what content they discuss, and whether and how they employ *teacher talk*. Students can refer to Egbert (1992) and Foley (1989) for information.

DEVELOP LESSONS USING AUTHENTIC LANGUAGE

Students develop a teacher-led lesson in which ESL students work at their own levels with authentic language.

DEVELOP AGE-APPROPRIATE DISCUSSION TOPICS

Students list authentic topics that are age appropriate for their learners to talk about.

CONSIDER STANDARD ENGLISH

Students argue for and against the use of the term *standard English*.

NOTES ON CASE 8

Case 9. Reading Between the Lines

IDENTIFY THE ISSUES

MAJOR ISSUES
Reading, language and content, learning strategies

OTHER ISSUES
Reflective teaching practices, time management, skill integration, strategic competence, the language of academic texts, non-ESL teachers' practices

READINGS
The following readings, also listed in each volume's Case Resources section, can help students understand the case issues. The Case Resources section contains many other texts that can also inform students.

Anderson, N. J. (2002). *The role of metacognition in second language teaching and learning.* Washington, DC: ERIC Clearinghouse on Language and Linguistics. (ERIC Document Reproduction Service No. ED463659). Retrieved February 22, 2005, from http://www.cal.org/resources/digest/0110anderson.html

Brown, H. D. (2001). *Teaching by principles: An interactive approach to language pedagogy.* White Plains, NY: Longman.

Lessard-Clouston, M. (1997). Language learning strategies: An overview for L2 teachers. *Internet TESL Journal, 3*(12). Retrieved February 5, 2005, from http://iteslj.org/Articles/Lessard-Clouston-Strategy.html

DISCUSS THE ISSUES

Positive Aspects
- The teacher has clear objectives that appear to be obtainable.
- The teacher is flexible and makes changes when needed.
- The teachers uses many different activities.
- There is a match between teaching and assessment.
- The goals are important.

Negative Aspects
- The teacher has started an ambitious program without enough information about how it will work.
- The students may not be familiar with many of the tasks.
- The content-area teachers do not appear to be addressing students' needs.

CONSIDER ALL PERSPECTIVES
Students might mention the perspectives of the ESL students and the teacher. The content-area teachers and maybe even their students are also affected by and affect the issues.

IDENTIFY RELEVANT PROFESSIONAL KNOWLEDGE

Students can check the readings mentioned previously, ESL methods texts, articles and books on reading, and research on learning strategies.

CONSIDER POSSIBLE ACTIONS AND CONSEQUENCES

The teacher could take some or none of the following actions and suffer some or none of the following consequences.

Action	Consequences
Complain to the content-area instructors.	The teacher earns the animosity of the content instructors.
	The content-area instructors become aware of what the ESL teacher thinks the solution should be.
Offer to help content-area instructors with strategy teaching.	The content-area instructors do not believe that this is their job and become angry or resentful.
	The content-area instructors are happy to collaborate.
	The students benefit from all of the teachers working toward this goal.
Teach only the four skill areas.	Students do not learn new strategies.
	Students' reading does not improve.
	Some students like class better.
Spend more time experimenting with different tasks and activities.	The teacher discovers more effective techniques.
	The teacher wastes time and effort.
	The students are confused.

CLOSURE: QUESTIONS FOR REFLECTION
- Summarize the class's analysis of the case.
- Present questions for current or future reflection. (See the case book for Reflection Questions.)

SUGGESTED ACTIVITIES

These activities can be used individually or together.

CONSIDER A SUBJECT-AREA TEXT

Students choose a subject-area text that is suitable for their students' level and highlight elements that might pose problems for English language learners.

CREATE TEXT SETS

Students use a subject-area text or topic that is commonly used and create text sets (parallel content and concepts at different levels).

DEVELOP TECHNIQUES TO IMPROVE ADULT READING

Students list other techniques that might help adult student reading achievement.

Case 10. The Subject of Language

IDENTIFY THE ISSUES

MAJOR ISSUES

English language learners' writing, 6+1 traits, genres of disciplines

OTHER ISSUES

Writing goals, students as models, using technology for language learning

READINGS

The following readings, also listed in each volume's Case Resources section, can help students understand the case issues. The Case Resources section contains many other texts that can also inform students.

Butler-Pascoe, M. E., & Wiburg, K. M. (2003). *Technology and teaching English learners.* Boston: Allyn & Bacon.

Byrd, P., & Reid, J. M. (1998). *Grammar in the composition classroom: Essays on teaching ESL for college-bound students.* New York: Heinle & Heinle.

Crandall, J., & Kaufman, D. (Eds.). (2002). *Content-based instruction in higher education settings.* Alexandria, VA: TESOL.

Larsen-Freeman, D. (2000). *Techniques and principles in language teaching* (3rd ed.). Oxford, England: Oxford University Press.

DISCUSS THE ISSUES

Positive Aspects
- The teacher is integrating research into his classes, and he is familiar with new ideas in the field.
- The teacher is following the program's curriculum.
- The teacher uses tools that he already has and knows well.
- The teacher uses a variety of resources and technologies.
- The teacher uses structures to help students organize their ideas.

Negative Aspects
- The teacher assumes that students will understand the differences between discourses.
- The teacher does not address his concern about the level of understanding.
- The teacher does not have a plan for building background knowledge about the idea of different discourses.
- The teacher has students working with outside experts whom he does not know and who may not be able to help in the same ways.

CONSIDER ALL PERSPECTIVES

Students might mention the stakes of the ESL students and perhaps the teacher. Less direct stakeholders are the subject-area teachers and experts in the professions with whom the students will interact.

IDENTIFY RELEVANT PROFESSIONAL KNOWLEDGE

Students can refer to the readings mentioned previously, ESL methods texts, and articles and books on genres, discourses, writing of English language learners, and second language acquisition.

CONSIDER POSSIBLE ACTIONS AND CONSEQUENCES

The teacher could take some or none of the following actions and suffer some or none of the following consequences.

Action	Consequences
Contact subject-area colleagues for collaboration.	The colleagues do not agree with the teacher's ideas.
	The colleagues do not know enough to help.
	The collaboration leads to benefits for the students and less work for the ESL teacher.
Prepare activities to help students activate prior knowledge.	Students benefit by understanding more.
	The teacher expends time and effort.
Do the unit as planned.	The teacher gets an idea of what works and what does not.
	The unit is a waste of time for the teacher and the students.
Decide not to work with genres because no one else does it.	The teacher disregards research that says working with genres is important.
	The students are underserved.
	The teacher saves time and effort.

QUESTIONS FOR REFLECTION
- Summarize the class's analysis of the case.
- Present questions for current or future reflection. (See the case book for Reflection Questions.)

SUGGESTED ACTIVITIES

These activities can be used individually or together.

EVALUATE A WRITING SAMPLE

Students go to the Northwest Regional Education Lab Web site (http://www.nwrel.org) and choose a writing sample from any appropriate grade level. They evaluate their sample and discuss the results and the process. This is a good way for teacher education students to understand how subjective writing grades can be.

COMPILE A CONTENT-AREA RESOURCES LIST

Students compile a content-area specific list of vocabulary, structures, and characteristics of genres used. They share their findings with the class.

DEVELOP AN ACTIVITY FOR TEACHING GENRES

Students develop another activity that could help the teacher teach content-area genres.

Case 11. Solving a Mystery

IDENTIFY THE ISSUES

MAJOR ISSUES
Technology in language learning, adult learners

OTHER ISSUES
Interaction, critical thinking, metacognition, student perceptions

Readings
The following readings, also listed in each volume's Case Resources section, can help students understand the case issues. The Case Resources section contains many other texts that can also inform students.

Egbert, J., & Hanson-Smith, E. (Eds.). (1999). *CALL environments: Research, practice, and critical issues.* Alexandria, VA: TESOL.

Kinoshita, C. Y. (2003). Integrating language learning strategy instruction into ESL/EFL lessons. *The Internet TESL Journal, 9*(4). Retrieved February 5, 2005, from http://iteslj.org /Techniques/Kinoshita-Strategy.html

Larsen-Freeman, D. (2000). *Techniques and principles in language teaching* (3rd ed.). Oxford, England: Oxford University Press.

DISCUSS THE ISSUES

Positive Aspects
- The activity is creative, and students seem motivated.
- Students have roles so that each contributes to the outcome.
- Scaffolding is provided, and reflection is encouraged.

Negative Aspects
- The teacher did not consider students' potential concerns.
- These kinds of activities have high dropout rates and take time to plan and maintain.
- Students' excitement might prevent them from accomplishing other tasks.

CONSIDER ALL PERSPECTIVES
Students might mention the stakes of the ESL students, the teacher, the parents, and the administrator. Less direct stakeholders are the students in the companion class.

IDENTIFY RELEVANT PROFESSIONAL KNOWLEDGE
Students can refer to the readings mentioned previously, ESL methods texts, and articles and books on computer-assisted language learning and adult education.

CONSIDER POSSIBLE ACTIONS AND CONSEQUENCES

The teacher could take some or none of the following actions and suffer some or none of the following consequences.

Action	Consequences
The teacher says that she's the expert and will not be challenged.	Other stakeholders get angry. Beneficial dialogue ends. The teacher risks losing her job and hurting her students.
Explain the research to the department chair.	Specific questions are not answered. The chair understands that the teacher's activity has a theoretical basis.
Show student examples of work.	Everyone understands the exact parameters of the task. The administrator asks for the activity to stop.
Agree to stop doing the activity.	This action avoids the problem. A motivating and effective learning experience for the students is taken away.
Discuss the task with the students.	Students understand the goals and background of the activity. Students are able to voice their concerns. The discussion digresses into other things that students like and do not like about the class.

CLOSURE: QUESTIONS FOR REFLECTION
- Summarize the class's analysis of the case.
- Present questions for current or future reflection. (See the case book for Reflection Questions.)

SUGGESTED ACTIVITIES

These activities can be used individually or together.

INCORPORATE TECHNOLOGY

Students add technology to a lesson they have written. They explain why and how it is appropriate and effective (or not).

ROLE-PLAY, TAKE 1

Students role-play the meeting between the teacher and the chair or the teacher discussing the class with the students.

ROLE-PLAY, TAKE 2

Students try the first role-play in a different content area with ESL students.

Case 12. A Process of Evaluation

IDENTIFY THE ISSUES

MAJOR ISSUES

English for specific purposes (ESP), mandated assessments, goals of assessment, types of assessment, authentic assessment, impact of assessment on students, predictive ability of assessments

OTHER ISSUES

Match between teaching and testing, authenticity of assessment, characteristics of good assessments, decision-making processes

READINGS

The following readings, also listed in each volume's Case Resources section, can help students understand the case issues. The Case Resources section contains many other texts that can also inform students.

Chapelle, C. A., & Stoynoff, S. (2005). *ESOL tests and testing: A resource for teachers and administrators.* Alexandria, VA: TESOL.

Coombe, C., & Hubley, N. (Eds.). (2003). *Assessment practices.* Alexandria, VA: TESOL.

O'Malley, J. M., & Pierce, L. V. (1996). *Authentic assessment for English language learners: Practical approaches for teachers.* New York: Addison-Wesley.

DISCUSS THE ISSUES

Positive Aspects
- The committee seems to be working well together and making visible progress toward agreeing on goals.
- The committee seems to understand assessment.

Negative Aspects
- Pleasing the company seems to be the priority.
- Committee members are working within many constraints.
- The committee's list of goals is fairly extensive and rules out numerous types of assessment before they can be fully considered.
- The committee members have not yet started to talk about the stakeholders and the purposes for these programs and assessments.
- The committee goals may be at odds with other stakeholders' goals.

CONSIDER ALL PERSPECTIVES

Students might mention the stakes of the company, the ESL students, and the teachers on the committee as those directly affected. They may also mention the chair as a major stakeholder.

IDENTIFY RELEVANT PROFESSIONAL KNOWLEDGE

Students can refer to the readings mentioned previously, ESL methods texts and articles, and books on the assessment of adult English language learners (particularly in their state or district) and ESP.

CONSIDER POSSIBLE ACTIONS AND CONSEQUENCES

The committee could take some or none of the following actions and suffer some or none of the following consequences:

Action	Consequences
Suggest keeping the assessment process the same.	No one invests additional time or funding.
	The problem is not solved.
	There is a mismatch between course content and assessment.
Suggest relying on the ESL teachers to decide how to assess their own students.	A more thorough assessment is allowed.
	Assessment becomes very inconsistent and subjective.
	Teachers have difficulty providing hard numbers regarding assessment results to the company.
Meet with the workers and the company to discuss ideas.	The teachers and the workers disagree.
	Everyone clarifies goals.
	The committee does not want to develop the classes.

CLOSURE: QUESTIONS FOR REFLECTION

- Summarize the class's analysis of the case.
- Present questions for current or future reflection. (See the case book for Reflection Questions.)

SUGGESTED ACTIVITIES

These activities can be used individually or together.

USE DIFFERENT MODES OF ASSESSMENT

Experiment with assessing the same activity in different ways. For example, provide students with an assignment written by an English language learner. Give each group of students a different rubric or criteria on which to assess the writing. How do the results differ? What do these differences suggest about the assessment criteria?

ROLE-PLAY

Students take on the role of the chair and reflect on the political, financial, or other considerations the chair might have to bear in mind. How can she please all the stakeholders? Students can write or give a short speech explaining her position to the college dean or the company representative.

RESEARCH LOCAL ESP PROGRAMS

Examine ESP programs in your area. How are they conducted? What do their curricula emphasize? What are their goals and outcomes?

Case 13. Homework

IDENTIFY THE ISSUES

MAJOR ISSUES
The use of classroom inquiry, culture, advocacy

OTHER ISSUES
Networking among ESL professionals, relationships between community, family, and teacher

READINGS
The following readings, also listed in each volume's Case Resources section, can help students understand the case issues. The Case Resources section contains many other texts that can also inform students.

Hubbard, R. S., & Power, B. M. (2003). *The art of classroom inquiry: A handbook for teacher-researchers* (Rev. ed.). Portsmouth, NH: Heinemann.

Schmuck, R. (1997). *Practical action research for change.* Arlington Heights, IL: Skylight.

Wrigley, H. S. (1993a). *Adult ESL literacy: Findings from a national study.* Washington, DC: National Clearinghouse for ESL Literacy Education. (ERIC Document Reproduction Service No. ED365169). Retrieved February 5, 2005, from http://www.ericdigests.org/1994/adult.htm

DISCUSS THE ISSUES

Positive Aspects
- The teacher is asking for help from members of the professional community and students.
- The teacher uses existing literature to inform practice.
- The teacher acts on her knowledge that different cultures approach things differently.

Negative Aspects
- The teacher is assuming that her students' children can respond effectively to the questions she wants to ask.
- The teacher assumes that the family members who agree to participate will also answer her questions.

Questions to Consider
- What could the teacher do if no one agrees to participate?
- Why might the teacher want family members to become more involved in the program?
- How might she get community buy-in for her advocacy?

CONSIDER ALL PERSPECTIVES
Students might mention the perspectives of the teacher, the practicum instructor, and the family members. Stakeholders also include the English language learners.

IDENTIFY RELEVANT PROFESSIONAL KNOWLEDGE

Students can refer to the readings mentioned previously, ESL methods texts, and articles and books on culture, community, education, and teacher inquiry.

CONSIDER POSSIBLE ACTIONS AND CONSEQUENCES

The practicum instructor could take some or none of the following actions and suffer some or none of the following consequences.

Action	Consequences
Tell the teacher how to advocate.	The teacher is not allowed to learn by discovering.
	The teacher has a place to start.
	The suggestions may not fit the teacher's context.
Tell the teacher that advocacy is not her job.	The research and good thinking that the teacher has done are ignored.
	The teacher does not reformulate or improve her ideas.
	The teacher is not supported in what she feels strongly about.
Discuss the project with the teacher.	The instructor understands the teacher's specific goals and ideas.
	The teacher is able to think through different aspects of her idea and think about how to approach advocacy so that it works.

CLOSURE: QUESTIONS FOR REFLECTION
- Summarize the class's analysis of the case.
- Present questions for current or future reflection. (See the case book for Reflection Questions.)

SUGGESTED ACTIVITIES

These activities can be used individually or together.

ROLE-PLAY

Students take the role of classroom instructor and write down questions they have for the teacher about her project. Have a question-and-answer session with one or more students portraying the teacher.

RESEARCH THE STUDENTS' CULTURES

Students suggest where the teacher might look for more information about her students and their cultures. What kinds of information should she look for, and how should she use it?

CREATE A WORKSHOP

Students outline a workshop for families about the ESL program. What should be included? How should it be presented?

BRAINSTORM

Students brainstorm ways to help nonnative-English-speaking families become more involved in the schooling of their adult members.

Case 14. So-Called Expert

IDENTIFY THE ISSUES

MAJOR ISSUES

The impact of demographic changes on programs and classrooms, types of ESL programs, characteristics of programs

OTHER ISSUES

Data gathering, resources needed for programs, program choice, skills versus themes

READINGS

The following readings, also listed in each volume's Case Resources section, can help students understand the case issues. The Case Resources section contains many other texts that can also inform students.

Echevarria, J., Vogt, M. E., & Short, D. (2004). *Making content comprehensible for English language learners: The SIOP model* (2nd ed.). Boston: Allyn & Bacon.

Ernst, G. (1994). Beyond language: The many components of an ESL program. *Anthropology and Education Quarterly*, *25*(3), 200–207.

McKeon, D. (1987). *Different types of ESL programs*. Washington, DC: ERIC Clearinghouse on Languages and Linguistics. (ERIC Document Reproduction Service No. ED289360). Retrieved February 5, 2005, from http://www.ericdigests.org/pre-927/types.htm

DISCUSS THE ISSUES

Positive Aspects
- The teacher uses many resources to help him decide.
- The teacher realizes that no program has hard and fast rules but that he can change and adapt it to fit the context.

Negative Aspects
- The teacher is conflicted about what he thinks is the best solution.
- The teacher might need more information about the benefits and disadvantages of different programs.
- The students were not consulted.

Questions to Consider
- How can the teacher recommend a program that will survive demographic changes?
- Where can the teacher find accurate demographic information?

CONSIDER ALL PERSPECTIVES

Students might mention that the direct stakeholders include the teachers and possibly the ESL students. Indirect stakeholders include the agency and possibly the English language learners' families.

IDENTIFY RELEVANT PROFESSIONAL KNOWLEDGE

Students can check the readings mentioned previously, ESL methods texts, articles and books on ESL programs, and statistics on local and national demographic changes and projections posted on the Internet.

CONSIDER POSSIBLE ACTIONS AND CONSEQUENCES

The teacher in this case could take some or none of the following actions and suffer some or none of the following consequences.

Action	Consequences
Recommend a skills-based program.	Students study the language rather than through the language.
	Some of the students are happy, but others are not.
Discuss further with colleagues and students.	Everyone can voice his or her opinions.
	Everyone thoroughly understands the choices.
	The decision is biased by other local programs.
Recommend the thematic program.	Some of the students are happy, but others disagree.
	The needs of English language learners are not met.
	Students' needs are met more fully than with a skills program.
Gather more evidence.	Stakeholders are encouraged to buy in to the program.
	Issues are clarified.
	More time and money is needed.
Integrate skills into themes.	The needs of different kinds of learners are addressed.
	Learning through and about language is included.
	Study time is more interesting.

CLOSURE: QUESTIONS FOR REFLECTION
- Summarize the class's analysis of the case.
- Present questions for current or future reflection. (See the case book for Reflection Questions.)

SUGGESTED ACTIVITIES

These activities can be used individually or together.

BRAINSTORM

Students brainstorm ways to develop better programs based on the literature, their experiences, and other resources. Barring money and time constraints, what would the ideal program look like? Compile a unified program from suggestions by small groups.

DEVELOP A PROGRAM CHART

In groups, students complete a program chart in a format similar to the one below. They can use interviews, general information about program types, and cases that describe actual implementations of programs.

Program Type	Cost per student	Staffing	Structure	Student population	Methods	Assessments

ROLE-PLAY

Students role-play a committee meeting in which they are talking to invited guests, taking on roles like the following:

- the teacher
- an agency representative
- a colleague who supports skills-based teaching and learning
- a colleague who supports themes
- a student who wants to learn English as quickly as possible
- a student who wants to maintain her first language
- an expert in whole language

Case 15. Create Your Own Case

This case is explained in the student books. The instructor can develop a rubric with the help of the students to guide the students' work and serve as an evaluation tool; alternately, students can share their cases and concerns, prepare activities to use their cases with their classmates, or develop other activities for this case.

Closure. What Have You Learned?

At the end of the course, the instructor might gather student reflections on what they have learned from participating in the case process. The teacher can gather this information using a formal evaluation, such as a report, or a less formal conversation with discussion points such the following:

- What do you see as the benefits of the case approach?
- What did you like about it?
- What did you dislike about it?
- What did you learn or think about by using this method that you might not have considered otherwise?
- What are the disadvantages of this approach?
- How would you do it differently? In what ways could it be more beneficial for you?

Also available from TESOL

Implementing the ESL Standards for Pre-K–12 Students Through Teacher Education
Marguerite Ann Snow, Editor

Integrating the ESL Standards Into Classroom Practice: Grades Pre-K–12
Betty Ansin Smallwood, Editor

Integrating the ESL Standards Into Classroom Practice: Grades 3–5
Katharine Davies Samway, Editor

Integrating the ESL Standards Into Classroom Practice: Grades 6–8
Suzanne Irujo, Editor

Integrating the ESL Standards Into Classroom Practice: Grades 9–12
Barbara Agor, Editor

Interaction and Language Learning
Jill Burton and Charles Clennell, Editors

Journal Writing
Jill Burton and Michael Carroll, Editors

Mainstreaming
Effie Cochran, Editor

Professional Development in Language Education
Volume 1. Becoming Contributing Professionals
Joy Egbert, Editor

Professional Development in Language Education
Volume 2. Extending Professional Contributions
Tim Murphey, Editor

Professional Development in Language Education
Volume 3. Sustaining Professionalism
Patricia Byrd and Gayle Nelson, Editors

Professional Development in Language Education
Volume 4. Communities of Supportive Professionals
Tim Murphey and Kazuyoshi Sato, Editors

Training Others to Use the ESL Standards: A Professional Development Manual
Deborah J. Short, Emily Lynch Gómez, Nancy Cloud,
Ann Katz, Margo Gottlieb, and Margaret Malone, Editors

For more information, contact
Teachers of English to Speakers of Other Languages, Inc.
700 South Washington Street, Suite 200
Alexandria, Virginia 22314 USA
Tel 703-836-0774 • Fax 703-836-6447 • publications@tesol.org
http://www.tesol.org/